THE TIGER AND THE MONKEY

by Sheryl Webster and Lera Munoz

"I am sleepy," said Tiger.

She went to sleep under a big tree.

A little monkey was eating nuts.

A nut fell from the tree.

Tiger woke up.

"Got you!" said Tiger.

Monkey was scared.

"Please don't eat me," he said.

"Please let me go.

One day, I will help you!"

Tiger laughed and laughed.
"You are too little to help me," she said.
But she let Monkey go.
"Thank you, Tiger," said Monkey.

The next day, Tiger was walking along the path. She was laughing. She did not see the trap.

Snap! Bang!

Tiger was stuck in the trap.

"Help! I cannot get out," said Tiger.

9

Tiger was scared.

She roared and roared.

Monkey heard Tiger roaring.
"Tiger did not eat me," he said.
"I will go and help her."

Monkey swung through the trees.

He saw Tiger stuck in the trap.

"I will help you!" he said.

"But you are little," said Tiger.

"How can you help me?"

"Yes, I am little," said Monkey, "but I can help you."

Monkey pushed the handle and pulled on the door. Tiger was free.

"Thank you for helping me," said Tiger. "I am glad that I did not eat you!"

Story trail

Start at the beginning of the story trail. Ask your child to retell the story in their own words, pointing to each picture in turn to recall the sequence of events.

Start

Independent Reading

This series is designed to provide an opportunity for your child to read on their own. These notes are written for you to help your child choose a book and to read it independently.

In school, your child's teacher will often be using reading books which have been banded to support the process of learning to read. Use the book band colour your child is reading in school to help you make a good choice. *The Tiger and the Monkey* is a good choice for children reading at Green Band in their classroom to read independently. The aim of independent reading is to read this book with ease, so that your child enjoys the story and relates it to their own experiences.

About the book

When a monkey wakes Tiger up, he is sure that she will eat him. But Tiger lets Monkey go. Soon after, Monkey helps Tiger.

Before reading

Help your child to learn how to make good choices by asking: "Why did you choose this book? Why do you think you will enjoy it?" Look at the cover together and ask: "What do you think the story will be about?" Support your child to think of what they already know about the story context. Read the title aloud and ask: "What animals can you see on the cover? What are the differences between them?"

Remind your child that they can try to sound out the letters to make a word if they get stuck.

Decide together whether your child will read the story independently or read it aloud to you. When books are short, as at Green Band, your child may wish to do both!

During reading

If reading aloud, support your child if they hesitate or ask for help by telling them the word. Remind your child of what they know and what they can do independently. If reading to themselves, remind your child that they can come and ask for your help if stuck.

After reading

Support comprehension by asking your child to tell you about the story. Use the story trail to encourage your child to retell the story in the right sequence, in their own words.
Give your child a chance to respond to the story: "Did you have a favourite part? Why did Monkey help Tiger?"
Help your child think about the messages in the book that go beyond the story and ask: "How does Tiger feel at the end of the story? What lesson does Tiger learn?"

Extending learning

Think about the story with your child, and make comparisons with the story The Lion and the Mouse, if this story is known to them. Help your child understand the story structure by using the same story context and adding different elements. "Let's make up a new story about a small animal that helps a larger animal. Which animals would you choose? What happens in your story?"
In the classroom, your child's teacher may be reinforcing punctuation and how it informs the way we group words in sentences. On a few of the pages, ask your child to find the speech marks that show us where someone is talking and then read it aloud, making it sound like talking. Find the question marks and ask your child to practise the expression they use for asking questions.

Franklin Watts
First published in Great Britain in 2024
by Hodder and Stoughton
Copyright © Hodder and Stoughton, 2024

All rights reserved.

Series Editors: Jackie Hamley and Melanie Palmer
Series Advisors and Development Editors: Dr Sue Bodman
and Glen Franklin
Series Designers: Cathryn Gilbert and Peter Scoulding

A CIP catalogue record for this book is
available from the British Library.

ISBN 978 1 4451 8928 4 (hbk)
ISBN 978 1 4451 8929 1 (pbk)
ISBN 978 1 4451 9131 7 (ebook)

Printed in China

Franklin Watts
An imprint of
Hachette Children's Group
Part of Hodder and Stoughton
Carmelite House
50 Victoria Embankment
London EC4Y 0DZ

An Hachette UK Company
www.hachette.co.uk

www.reading-champion.co.uk